Harmonica for Beginners

Learn How to Play the Harmonica through Interactive Sheet Music, Engaging Audio Examples, and Comprehensive Narrations (Over 20 Audio Guides)

By: Oliver Dalton

Text Copyright © Lightbulb Publishing

All rights reserved. No part of this guide may be reproduced in any form without permission in writing from the publisher except in the case of brief quotations embodied in critical articles or reviews.

Legal & Disclaimer

The information in this book and its contents are not designed to replace or substitute any form of medical or professional advice. It is not intended to replace the need for independent medical, financial, legal, or other professional advice or services as may be required. The content and information in this book have been provided for educational and entertainment purposes only.

The content and information in this book have been compiled from reliable sources and are accurate to the best of the Author's knowledge, information, and belief. However, the Author cannot guarantee the accuracy and validity and cannot be held liable for errors and/or omissions. Furthermore, changes are made periodically to this book as and when needed.

Where appropriate and/or necessary, you must consult a professional (including but not limited to your doctor, attorney, financial advisor, or such other professional advisor) before using any of the suggested remedies, techniques, or information in this book.

Upon using the contents and information in this book, you agree to hold harmless the Author from and against any damages, costs, and expenses, including any legal fees potentially resulting from the application of any of the information provided. This disclaimer applies to any loss, damages, or injury caused by the use and application, whether directly or indirectly, of any advice or information presented, whether for breach of contract, tort, negligence, personal injury, criminal intent, or under any other cause of action.

You agree to accept all the risks of using the information presented in this book.

You agree by continuing to read this book that, where appropriate and/or necessary, you shall consult a professional (including but not limited to your doctor, attorney, financial advisor, or such other advisor as needed) before using any of the suggested remedies, techniques, or information in this book.

Table of Contents

Chapter 1: Introduction 1

Chapter 2: Getting to Know the Harmonica 5

Chapter 3: Let's Play Some Harmonica! 15

Chapter 4: Understanding Rhythm and Beat 29

Chapter 5: A Closer Look At Notes..37

Chapter 6: Crossharp..45

Chapter 7: Harmonica Techniques...53

Chapter 8: Jamming With Your Harmonica 63

Chapter 9: Deep Cleaning, Repair, and Conclusion......................69

Throughout this book there are musical examples and audio recordings to follow along with on your journey to learn how to play the harmonica.

Whenever you see the following outline or similar:

> 🔊
>
> **1. Harmonica Keys**

Please follow along with the recordings at the following website: https://bit.ly/3IUHkhc

Or Scan the QR Code:

Chapter 1

Introduction

The harmonica is one of the easiest and most portable instruments to play! Whether you have no musical knowledge or want to add the harmonica to your repertoire, you can find the basics here to get you going. This book will teach you how to play songs, jam with other musicians, and tips on improvisation. Just remember that it is up to you to practice! There are no shortcuts to playing the harmonica, just repetitive playing and listening.

A Brief History of the Harmonica

The harmonica belongs to the free reed aerophone family. These are instruments that create their sound by air vibrating over reeds. There are a variety of instruments in this family, such as accordion, pump organs, harmonium, pitch pipes, and sheng from China. They are similar to woodwinds except for the wind or breath isn't blown into a tube. The harmonica itself was invented by multiple people during the 19th century when an array of new instruments was created in Europe. Different "mouth harp" patents were arriving on the scene about 20 years before Adolphe Sax invented the saxophone.

It's normal for instruments and songs to have more than one inventor or origin. The very nature of music is mimicry, and when we hear something we like, there is a drive to copy it! Which means tracing the history and origin of said music can be a difficult trail to follow. Early harmonicas were inspired by the sheng, and they were also used as pitch pipes to tune pianos. Joseph Richter invented a method to blow and draw air across the reed for two different notes, which gave the instrument more variety. It became popular in Bohemia and Germany, where the construction was streamlined.

The German city of Trossingen was an important part of harmonica history thanks to the makers Charles Messner and Matthias Hohner. You may very well have a Hohner harmonica on you now, as that company is still one of the prominent manufacturers of the instrument. These builders began creating metal stamps for the reeds and mass-producing wood combs so that more people could buy their products. By the end of the 19th century, the harmonica was becoming popular, and new variations were invented. However, the diatonic or one-key style was the easiest and most sought after by potential players. There was also a harmonica factory in Klingenthal, which was the home of the Seydel model. Many of the modern aspects of the harmonica were created or perfected in southern Germany, as that region was a hot spot for music in the 18th and 19th centuries.

Immigrants from Europe then took their harmonicas and brought them to the U.S., where they quickly took hold in folk and blues styles. New playing techniques were created, and the harmonica began appearing in records, and even a radio show called the *Hohner Harmony Hour*. However, it was still associated with the poor, so it was hard to break into mainstream music with it. Once World War II started, its popularity decreased because of its association with Germany and its roots in Asia. But with the advent of Rhythm and Blues (which would later be named

Introduction

Rock'n'roll), the instrument found its modern home. People use harmonicas in jazz, orchestra, pop, and even classical, but the blues, rock, and folk are where you will find the most songs.

Artists like Bob Dylan, Neil Young, and Stevie Wonder (who played a chromatic harp) used the harmonica on many record hits, giving the instrument a larger status. They didn't use it in the whole song, usually only for intros and solos, much like a lead guitarist would do. This made it so more listeners who bought their records also purchased harmonicas to play. The idolization of rock stars and celebrities helped the instrument gain a little more credibility. Like the ukulele or recorder, the harmonica is often labeled a toy, which can lead to many musicians dismissing it for any serious purpose. Thankfully, famous performers showed the world how great it can be!

As you study and play the harmonica, it is important to look into more musicians and artists who have used it historically. When you find someone you like, take a deeper look into their song catalog and listen every day to memorize it. Besides harmonica history, it will also help to learn more about music in general, don't just be a harmonicist. Work on your greater ability to be a musician! When you are doom scrolling social media or stuck in a boredom loop, escape it by seeking out new music. Listen to new styles, genres, and artists, and even keep a journal of what you like and new ideas. The main reason many musicians fail is that they do not totally immerse themselves in the process. Do not worry about how good you are. Just play, listen, and learn to play better with each practice.

Remember

- The harmonica has roots across Asia and Central Europe, people have been using aerophone-reed instruments for thousands of years.

- Oftentimes, the most famous harmonica players are multi-instrumentalists, vocalists, and songwriters. It is often seen as an additional instrument as opposed to a stand-alone like a piano.

- How well you succeed at this process of playing the harmonica will all depend upon how much you immerse yourself in music. Even if this is just a fun hobby, your best results are achieved through daily practice.

Trivia

- The harmonica is the most bought instrument in the world, but many players do not follow through with it.

- It was also the first instrument to be brought into space as it is so portable.

- The harmonica has many names, such as the blues harp, French harp, mouth organ, tin sandwich, pocket piano, Mississippi saxophone, gob iron, and pocket orchestra, among many more!

Chapter 2

Getting to Know the Harmonica

Topics Covered

- How to buy a harmonica

- Harmonica anatomy

- How sound is produced

- What are keys and which do you need

- Basic care for your harmonica

In this book, we will be studying and playing the diatonic harp. It is smaller, cheaper, and easier to play than chromatics. With the skills you learn, it will eventually be possible to play other models, but first, start with the standard 10-hole diatonic or blues harp harmonica. The chromatic is larger and has a button to press to change your notes, while the diatonic lacks this.

Purchasing a Harmonica

Buying a harmonica is not as big of a purchase as buying other instruments, but you still have to take the same precautions. If you do not spend the right amount of money, you will end up with an unplayable toy. One of the most common reasons for musical failure is trying to learn on an instrument that does not have correct intonation, which means the notes will sound as they should. No matter how hard you try, you cannot succeed with poor intonation or broken reeds. Try to stick to budgets above $50 for a higher quality instrument, as it is worth the money to start with something nice. It's also wise to avoid an expensive pro model until you know you will enjoy it. Be realistic in that it's a new hobby, so spend a modest amount without going too high or low!

Another instrument that is essential in your music journey is a piano/keyboard, which can be downloaded from a digital app if necessary. If you have a piano or physical keyboard, that's great.

Otherwise, low-cost software or apps will also suit your needs. It doesn't have to be fancy. It just helps tremendously if you can see and hear the notes as we discuss them in the book. No matter what instrument you play, comparing your study to piano sounds and keys will help you advance faster than other students. Don't think of it as learning two instruments. The keyboard is just there to help guide you. If you happen to play guitar, ukulele, or any other instrument, you can also use them in your studies. Music is all about the big picture, and once you can see the many concepts will start to click.

Usually, in music, it's normal to wait a few lessons before diving into theory, but with the diatonic harmonica, we need to understand what a key is! On a piano, there are 12 notes that are a semitone apart, and each one has a major scale. As such, there are 12 different harmonicas to match each key. If you want to play with backing tracks that have more than drums it is important to know the key of your harmonica. The best and most common key to start with is C major. Otherwise, many students will have G, D, A, and E.

The key of the harmonica is on the side, and if not, you will need to use a tuner app on your phone (some are simple and free but complicated ones cost more). If you get an old-fashioned tuner, make sure it is chromatic so you can see whatever notes you are playing. If you blow the holes numbered 1 or 4 into a tuner it will show the main note and key. As you learn to play the harmonica the tuner will come in handy for checking your progress and tone. Music is all about listening, so the more you analyze the notes critically, the better you will do!

🔊 1. Harmonica Keys

Some students wonder if it is ok to buy used harmonicas, and the answer is yes, as long they are in reasonable shape. At the end of this book there are instructions and photos on how to give the harmonica a deep clean for situations where they need it! For those players who want multiple keys, buying used is one way to save money as long as they can be properly cleaned. If the instrument is intonated right, you can go for new or used. Playability is what it all comes down to. Now, let's take a look at the inside of the harmonica and see what causes it to play correctly or not!

Harmonica Anatomy

This is the standard 10-hole diatonic harmonica in the key of C. It has a middle wooden comb, two brass reed plates, and two outer pieces that are usually metal but can also be plastic. The important part is the reed plates and that they all sound right. Many modern harmonicas can have plastic or resin combs, but they are not always wood.

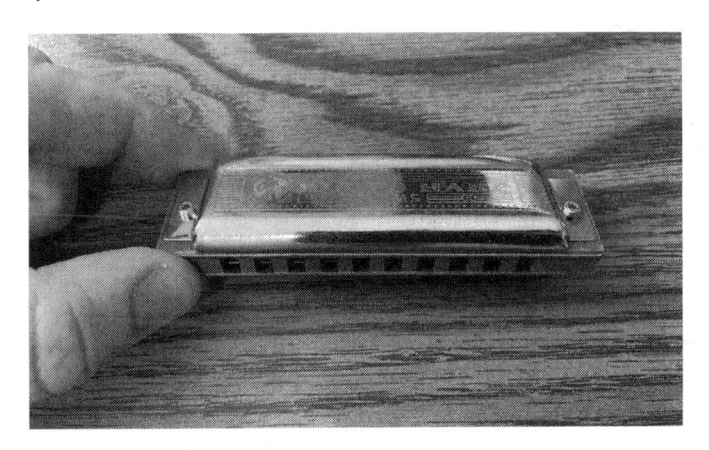

Once you take the covers off, the reed plates are exposed. 10 reeds are faced inward on the top for blowing air, and 10 more reeds are faced outward on the bottom for drawing air. The wooden comb has 10 slots to hold all these reeds and gives them a space for air to pass, allowing vibration. Once the reeds vibrate, the thin brass resonates, and you get that distinct harmonica sound.

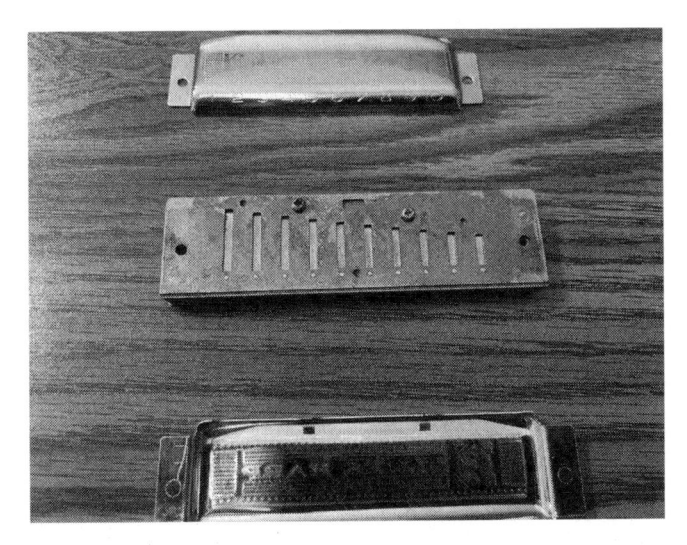

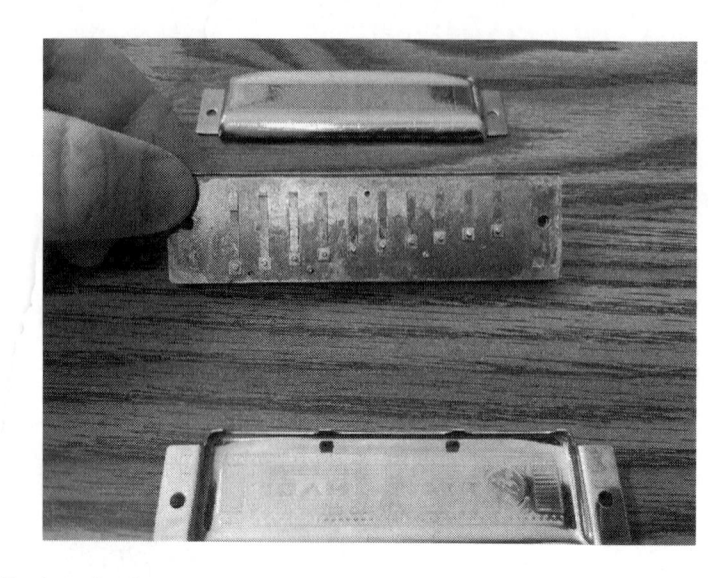

Notice the brass is not perfectly shiny. This harmonica is nearly two decades old! However, it still plays great and has no dirt or debris in it. Even new harps will show a degree of tarnished brass after a brief period of use. As long as those reeds are in great shape, there is no reason to stress on discoloration. The wood comb, however, is one reason we need to do regular basic cleaning, as it can get quite dirty with buildup.

As mentioned, some combs are made with plastic, wood resin, and other composite materials. In that case, it may last longer, but you still have to keep it clear. Remember you are essentially blowing air and spit into the instrument so it will be necessary to knock the debris and saliva out when finished. You just simply take the harmonica and knock the holes across your hand or a towel. The motion also helps pass air through the harmonica to dry it. Deep cleans are something you do rarely, as long as you keep up this habit.

Now look and see how the reeds are barely above the plate, if you do take your harmonica apart this is where you have to tread carefully. You don't want to bend, scrape, or get anything lodged underneath these tiny reeds. It is possible to order replacements and install them, as long as each reed is tuned to the right note. On this C harmonica the image below shows every note that is blown and drawn through each hole. Individual harmonica keys will have a different set of notes depending on what makes up their major scale.

C	E	G	C	E	G	C	E	G	C
1	2	3	4	5	6	7	8	9	10
D	G	B	D	F	A	B	D	F	A

On a diatonic harmonica no matter where we blow, we will be playing the notes that make up the major chord. If you have already begun playing around, you have likely noticed that it always sounds pleasant or consonant even if you blow multiple holes. However, if you suck or draw air in sometimes it sounds bad or dissonant. The notes of the C major scale are C D E F G A B which you can see move in that order from hole 4 to hole 7. The low holes do not go in order as they are for chords, while the middle is for melodies, and the high end is for embellishment. If you are not playing a C harp that is ok, the basic songs and riffs we first learn will still work.

Harmonica tablature is a way to read music for new students who may not yet know standard sheet music. It can work in a variety of ways, but the main goal is to label the hole played and whether the air is (B)lown or (D)rawn. Sometimes arrows are used, circles, or just letters like below. The major scale on the harmonica follows this pattern.

4(B) 4(D) 5(B) 5(D) 6(B) 6(D) 7(D) 7(B)

Notice how it changes at the 7 hole as the root note needs to be the blown one. It is likely a struggle at this point to hit single holes and that is normal for beginners. In the next chapter we will start playing simple songs and working on our lip and single note skills. If you were playing at all, remember to give the harmonica some knocks against your palm and maybe a quick cloth shine to keep it clean. Little moments of care will make your instruments last for years!

2. Major Scale and Embouchure

Remember

- Your learning setup should be a harmonica, keyboard or piano for reference, and a chromatic tuner. This can be hardware or an app, whichever you prefer.

- There are 12 harmonicas for each key, to begin with it doesn't matter what you play but once you jam with others it will be important.

- Now that you know what it looks like in the harmonica it is easy to see how food and particles may get stuck so be sure to keep it clean.

Trivia

- John Popper of Blues Traveler invented a wearable suspender like contraption for all 12 keys. That way when he is on stage, he is ready for any song that may be played.

- Harmonicas are used by doctors and respiratory therapists to help exercise the lungs. Even though it is a simple instrument it takes a lot of wind to play it.

- Many harmonicas are toys and are not meant to be played musically. If it is in a department store or cheap bin it likely isn't playable, stick to proper music manufacturers.

Chapter 3

Let's Play Some Harmonica!

Topics Covered

- Your first harmonica song

- How to shape your mouth

- Breathing tips and exercises

- Embouchure and mouth shape

If you have already been experimenting with playing you may have found the breathing and single note playing to be more difficult than you expected. You will get winded after a few notes of blowing and drawing and that will be completely normal. It will also be common to hit errant notes, again this happens and the only way to overcome it is regular practice. We all sound bad at first, if necessary, go and find a private place to play where no one can hear you. Find a quiet, judgment free zone and get started!

Your First Harmonica Song

The traditional first song most harmonica players learn is "Oh Susanna" by Stephen Foster, first published way back in 1848! It's a minstrel song with lyrics that haven't aged well but the notes and rhythm are perfect for beginners. The melody is made up of the major pentatonic scale which is the easiest musical scale you can learn. Every note of the verse and chorus is covered by blowing and drawing holes 4, 5, and 6 along the major scale. Another great feature of this ditty is that you can be a little sloppy with your notes and it will still sound ok.

```
Verse

4-4    5    6    6-6   6   5
 I   came from Al-a-bam-a

4   -4  5   5   -4   4   -4
with my ban-jo on my knee

4-4    5    6   6   -6   6 5
I'm goin'  to Lou-'si-an-a

4-4    5    5   -4   -4   4
M-y  true love for  to  see.

4-4    5    6   6   -6   6  5   4
I-t rained all night the day I left

-4   5   5   -4   4   -4
The weath-er it was dry;

4  -4  5   6   6 -6   6    5    4
Th-e sun so hot I froze to death

-4  5  5    -4    -4   4
Su-san-na, don't you cry.

Chorus

-5   -5 -6  -6   -6    6   6   5   4   -4
Oh,  Su-san-na, oh, don't you cry for me

4  -4   5    6   6-6   6 5
I-ye come from Al-a-bam-a

4   -4  5  5   -4  -4   4
with my ban-jo on my knee.
```

🔊

3. Oh Susanna Tips

How did that go? If it went well, awesome, if not welcome to the club! You probably noticed within a few notes that you were out of breath, it was hard to play single notes, and maybe your lips were not moving that smoothly. It's important to find your weaknesses when playing so you know exactly what needs to be worked on. It doesn't take much on the exhale to create a nice sound, in fact you want to blow lightly so the tone stays steady and nice. When you inhale you may hear the sound "bending" if you suck hard or move your tongue. This is a process we will refine later to play new notes but for now keep your draw notes steady. A tuner will allow you to check that you are playing the correct note, keep playing it until it stays steady and sounds good.

"Straight harp" is where we play simple melodies that arise from the major scale, and these are the first songs most people play on their harmonica. It may seem simple and silly to learn traditional and kids songs but they are the best entry for all ages of musicians. It is also against copyright to share certain modern songs so a teacher cannot just go showing them without paying for the license. If you look up harmonica tabs online you may find them to be wrong and this is because the sites cannot legally share specific aspects. One famous song that recently left copyright to enter the public domain is "Happy Birthday to You." That song and a few other oldies are perfect melodies for the beginning harmonicist!

```
 6   6   -6    6   7 -7
Hap-py birth-day to you,

 6   6   -6    6  -8  7
Hap-py birth-day to you,

 6   6    9    8   7 -7  -6
Hap-py birth-day to  ___ ___

-9  -9    8    7  -8  7
Hap-py birth-day to you.
```

"Happy Birthday" will be hard as there are high notes that will shriek and squeal back at you! The purpose is to get you accustomed to those notes, not perfection. If a shrill sound occurs, stop, reset your mouth shape, and try again. Do not suck so much air in, just breathe normally. Now go look up some other traditional tunes that you may like whether they are kids, holiday, or silly songs. The better you know the song already in your head, the easier it will be. Some tabs may be confusing or too advanced, if so just move on to another. When you find a tab that you can play, make sure to save or print it for future practice. Don't just play what the teacher tells you to, work with what songs you like and know best!

In the next part we will be looking at mouth and breathing exercises but first here is a tip that will truly help you advance in your playing. In the old days people had amazing musical talent but there were no eBooks, blogs, online guides, or even many local teachers, so how did they do it? They used ear training and mimicry, which means they listened and then tried to copy. That's how it was done, you would put a record on and start trying to play along. It was tedious and very hard to do, but that is what makes a musician great. Listen to your mistakes and make changes to correct them and try playing as many songs as possible. Take the initiative to try music you like, don't worry about success and failure, just keep playing anything.

Mouth Shape and Lip Movement

Before we start working on our mouth shape the best way to hold the harmonica is between your index finger and thumb, cupped in the palm of your hand. You can use your left or right depending on what is most comfortable. Later we will use our other hand to form a sound hole but for now it is fine to do beginning techniques in this manner.

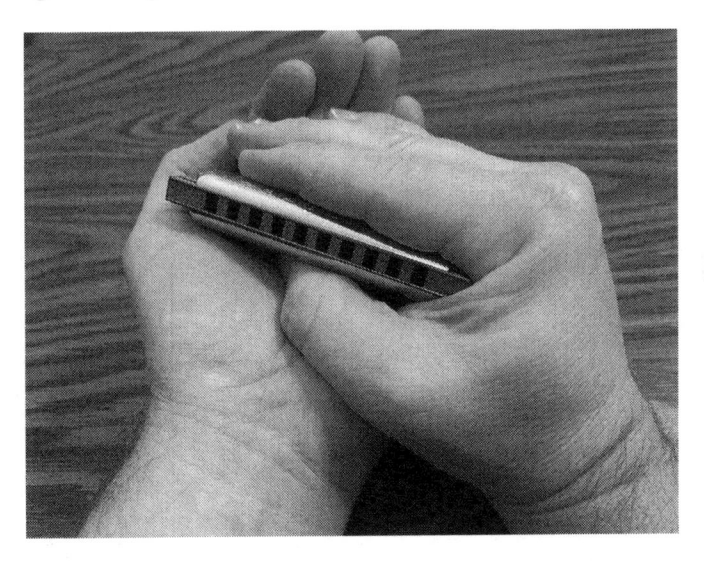

Your lips need to be moist but not soaking, we don't want too much saliva that it becomes detrimental or gross. If the lips are dry and chapped it will be hard to smoothly play or to get a proper tone out of the reeds. Next, we want to start working on our "pucker" skills, it's not quite the same pucker as when you kiss someone, but it is very close. Your lips need to form a round shape so that it is possible to play just one single note. Start by saying the vowel "oh" and then tighten up your lips to form a little circle of air to inhale and exhale with. Now you have the basic mouth shape, the next step is to place it in your mouth. Don't just barely touch it with your lips, push it into that pucker.

The more it pushes into your mouth the better tone you will be able to get, however don't press the pucker hard against the harmonica. Some players like to angle the harmonica upward as it helps form a tighter seal between the puckered lips. There needs to be a proper connection to keep air from releasing and to control the notes we want to eventually move to. If you struggle it is fine to pick any manner that allows you to play one hole at a time, sometimes people use their tongues. It also helps to cover all holes but one with your thumbs and then blow and draw to hear the clear single notes. Experiment with the best positions that allow you to have the right sound, if it doesn't assess what you have done wrong. When band students play brass or woodwinds they spend many hours in early practice on that embouchure, be sure to move your mouth around until you get the best sounds. The major scale and the songs above are great ways to work on proper mouth shape.

4(B) 4(D) 5(B) 5(D) 6(B) 6(D) 7(D) 7(B)

While you are working on hitting single hole notes try to play the major scale on the 4-7 holes. It will take some time to be able to comfortably play single notes but that is the goal. In the meantime, while you practice the scale you still have other techniques to learn. While you are playing the major scale or any song have you noticed your tongue wanting to move along with music at times. Hopefully you have, as we need to use our tongue to separate notes, mute, bend, and more as it can often be where the soul of the harmonica comes from. Just like when you talk and sing the tongue emotes and expresses more than most people realize, after all harmonica really is just an extension of vocals. While some inner mouth exercises are more advanced the first and easiest is tonguing.

When you say the "Tah" sound your tongue touches the roof of your mouth above your teeth. Say "tah, tah, tah, tah…" and pick the harmonica up and start playing at the same time. This will give you a *staccato* sound and make it so the notes are separated, initially the "tah" will be heard through the harmonica. However, with improvement the tongue should hit this spot lightly and silently unless you want a driving rhythm. We all have different mouth shapes so like the pucker it is important to find your sweet spot of where tonguing works the best.

4. Tongued Major Scale

At this point you should be able to sit back and work on extended practices where you play the major scale, example songs, or you simply jam and discover what sounds good and bad. Work on the pucker, tonguing, single notes, and move your tongue around to see what changes. Your practices should last 15-30 minutes and that will be hard at first. If you haven't noticed yet, the breathing aspect of this is rough! For the best chances of succeeding at the harmonica it is imperative to work on your breathing.

Breathing Breakthroughs

Besides practicing on a regular basis there are some great tips and techniques for breathing and building up your lung capacity. First off, some people play the harmonica as a way to improve their lung health and they aren't focused on wailing away to the blues. If you are a player that has had a respiratory illness there is no need to push yourself to problematic situations, play in moderation and keep your practices short. Our goal with proper breathing and training is more about getting a clear and constant tone instead of just being loud or powerful.

When you blow air, you should be pretending to fog up a mirror as opposed to using a straw, with the pucker you may have been doing that! Relax that pucker in the lips so the air flows out from the back of the mouth. When you draw air, raise the back of your throat like you are yawning, that is better than breathing through your nose. By blowing and drawing in these manners you are breathing through the harmonica as you play, use the nose for larger inhaling and exhaling when NOT playing. This will not be easy to control at first but one thing you for sure can change immediately is breathing from your diaphragm. Breathe deep and correctly so you get the most air you can.

Of course, exercise is going to be your best bet to breathing better and having more stamina. If you add simple things like walking to your routine it will benefit your harmonica playing and more intense cardio will help you emote. It's also helpful to use singers' exercises as you are really just a vocalist with reeds. Here are some common tips among musicians to breathe better and more efficiently.

- Put a piece of regular paper against the wall at head level and blow, see how long you can hold it up before it falls!

- Count to 4 and breathe in, once you get there draw two quick breaths in, exhale and do the same quick movement at the end. Once you are good at that, increase your count.

- Place your hands on your belly and chest and breathe as deep as you can. Watch, feel, and become more aware of how to breathe from your body.

- Vocalists will also breathe in silly ways like panting, through straws, and often lots of lip trills and movement to also warm the mouth up. The goal is to get the muscles moving and prepare the lungs.

Now that you have some mouth and breathing exercises hopefully your first songs above are getting easier. Before we look at some rhythmic techniques on the harmonica let's fix our overall tone with a better grip!

How to Hold the Harmonica

So far, our main concerns have been getting acquainted with the body and notes of the harmonica, but you will find with a better hold that you can get cleaner and louder sounds. There is no exact way to hold the harmonica and if you use a metal holder around your neck then you don't touch it at all! When a player wants a bluesy or soulful sound though it can help to cup your hands holding one behind the back of the harmonica. Below is a view from the front and back. You may hold the harmonica in either your left or right hand, it's all based on your comfort and control.

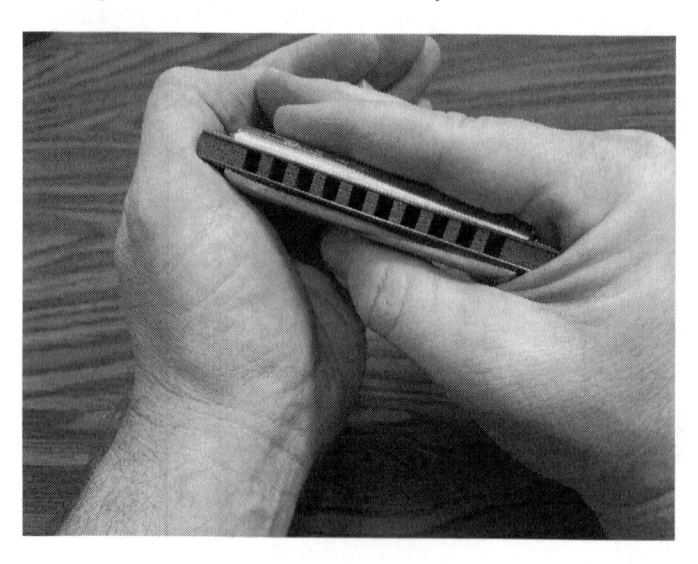

Let's Play Some Harmonica!

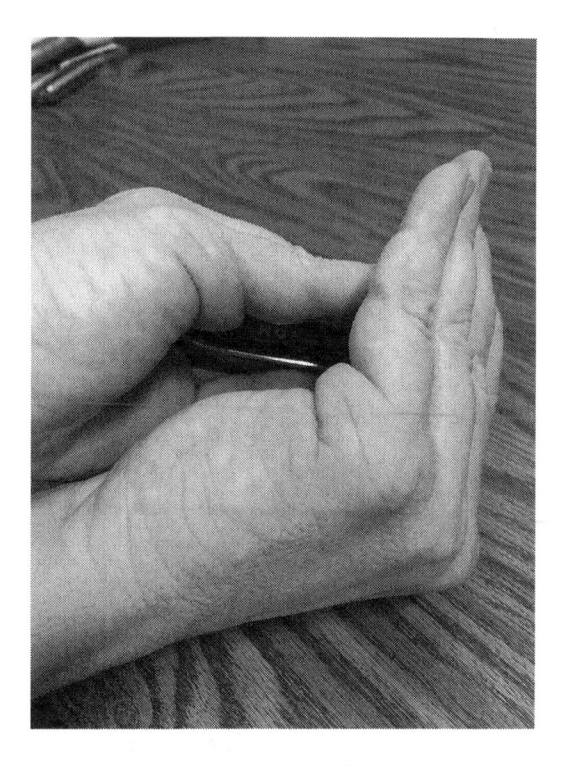

The pictures show the outer hand open; sometimes it will be closed, or it may be fluttered back and forth to create wailing or wah wah sound effects. If we start lightly blowing at hole 7 and then move down 6-5-4 and end on a C chord of 3-4-5 along with shaking our hand lightly, we will get a nice cowboy harmonica ending sound.

> 🔊
> **5. Cowboy Flutter Effect**

Because the harmonica is such a simple instrument, we need to use other parts of our body to enhance the tone and volume. Our mouth helps shape the sound, the tongue gives it definition, and the cupped hand movement provides an acoustic space like a guitar body. We need to look at all these parts as contributors to the vibe, emotion, and feeling of the harmonica instrument. As you play your first songs try to hone all of these movements to your own needs. At the same time, you want to copy what this book and other players say, this is a personal music maker that each grip and pucker is unique to everyone. This is one reason why practice is so essential so you can find what works best, maybe you need a different angle, or the harmonica has to be pushed deeper into the mouth.

Regardless of how much progress you have made you are at the point where you can start creating your own music. A necessary part of being a musician, so take a moment to compose your first harmonica song. Get a proper grip and play your single notes starting at hole 4. Tongue it with a couple blows and move to note 5 and shake your backing hand. It will probably be sloppy with multiple notes but that's ok, just play slow and give it emotion. Move up another note and tongue some more, imagine playing a slow Western tune. Songs are all about tension and resolution so after you build up to the higher notes end on the 4 hole again. This will be the first phrase of your tune!

🔊

6. Backing Track 1 Example

> 🔊
> **7. Backing Track 1 Pop Drums 90 BPM**

Since you are playing in one diatonic key it will be easy to avoid mistakes, some draw notes may sound off if more than one hole is played, if so just adjust your pucker. Play along with the major scale some more to enhance your melody and don't worry about perfection or rushing. Focus on fixing airy tones, loud breathing, lack of mouth control, and most of all keep working on the single note playing. You should be practicing every day, if you have trouble with stamina, you can do short bursts a few times a day. It's a very portable instrument, the goal is to always take the time to do it. In the next chapter we will start working on rhythms and some basic music theory on the beat.

Remember

- There are websites that have harmonica tabs of most songs, some are free, others paid. Browse different genres and music styles and try playing any you know. Find examples of the songs you choose to play along with.

- Some holes will be very hard to play. The 2 and 3 draw can take some time to play right. The high notes can also be a hassle so work on them occasionally while you perfect the middle 4-7 holes.

- Breathing is an essential part of harmonica playing, it will take time to improve your lungs to get through a song without running out of breath!

Trivia

- If you struggle to play a song it may be because you do not have the notes! Some famous tunes like Sesame Street and Stevie Wonder hits use a chromatic harp.

- Most songs enter the public domain after 75 years but that can vary. Once it is in the public domain you can record or cover it as you see fit.

- One of the fastest speeds ever played on harmonica was 103 notes in 20 seconds! Of course, we will never need to play this fast but what a feat!

Chapter 4

Understanding Rhythm and Beat

Topics Covered

- Popular Harmonica Rhythms
- What is the beat?
- Notes and timing
- Counting basic rhythms

The harmonica makes a great melody instrument, but you are likely struggling with single note playing so in the meantime we can look at the fundamental aspects of the beat and rhythm. In music the beat is the unit of time that way musicians can communicate how long a note lasts. For those who can read sheet music it tells us the length of each beat, otherwise we have to use our ears to listen!

Understanding the Beat

The beat can also be called the pulse, and it is easier to learn if we use a metronome and backing drum track. Like the piano apps there are many drum machines and metronomes that are affordable or even free. They will help you with practice, timing, and making sure you grasp the larger principles of rhythm. If we cannot play in the proper time frame it will sound just as bad as the wrong note, each beat has its place and time to make the song work! Beats are grouped into measures and the way they are divided up and played will help form their meter.

The most common meters we will see in our playing is 3/4 and 4/4, these time signatures are how we express our meters. 3/4 means there are 3 quarter beats per measure and 4/4 has 4 quarters per measure. Most meters are made up of 2 or 3 beat divisions, even if you advance into weird time signatures, they can always be broken up this way. The point of meters is to provide different feelings for our songs and compositions. If we play something in 3/4 time it sounds like a waltz with its 1-2-3, 1-2-3 and in 4/4 time it has a more even sound with its 1-2-3-4, 1-2-3-4. Many songs on the radio and streaming are in 4/4, it is called *common time* as it is the most used. Of the songs we have discussed so far Oh Susanna is in 4/4 while Happy Birthday is in 3/4.

> 🔊
> 8. 4/4 and 3/4 time

Music occurs because of a tension and release, just as notes change so does the beat. If we just play our metronome at 80 BPM it will get boring and annoying very fast as there is no variation for our ears to pick up on. By accenting and stressing certain beats we can change the vibe and groove of what we are playing. The first beat in a measure is the downbeat and the most important, especially if you play for James Brown. He is notorious for big downbeat hits that help bring out the funk. The beat after the

Understanding Rhythm and Beat

downbeat is the upbeat and these two move back and forth to create the tension and release. In 4/4 time the beats are counted 1-2-3-4 with the 1 and 3 as the down beat and the 2 and 4 as the upbeat, backbeat or off beat. As always music is filled with different ways to name concepts and depending on how we play these notes will give us a variety of genres!

Syncopation is where we accent, or stress certain beats more than others and it is what causes people to dance. If you listen to the beats of any uplifting or dancing genre you will notice they have certain points of stress in a rhythmic pattern. The most common you will see as a harmonica player is the blues backbeat. This is where we play One-**TWO**-Three-**FOUR**, that 2 and 4 offbeat are hit really hard on a snare drum to give us the blues and rock. You can simulate this by clapping your hands harder at those two offbeat notes. By putting the impetus and syncopation on different beats it causes more of a drive thus the reason rock is so popular, that beat manipulation is just too hard for most humans to resist. But that backbeat isn't all that makes rock and blues, we also need 1/8th notes played on the hi-hat cymbal. We create a more complex rhythm by subdividing and adding another set of beats in. Below are the basic divisions of the beat that we will mostly use.

Whole Note   Half Note   Quarter Note   Eighth Note

🔊 9. Metronome Accents

As you can see it is in common time and each measure has only 4 beats a piece. Play a single note like 4(B) as a whole note and count 1 2 3 4, next play two half notes at two beats a piece, and the easiest to do is the quarter notes with their basic 1-2-3-4. Try playing those quarter notes as staccato with your tah sound on the tongue. Now make a "la" shape and feel how your tongue touches the roof of your mouth lighter? The hard tah will help us play short and staccato while the "la" will give us a legato length, these are regular as notated above. We can further divide our quarter notes into eighth notes and count them in this manner.

1 + 2 + 3 + 4 +   1 + 2 + 3 + 4 +

🔊 10. Staccato Vs Legato

One reason the Christmas traditional "Jingle Bells" is a common teaching song is that it has an easy melody and great examples of basic note lengths. The quarter, half, and whole notes are perfectly laid out making the melody accessible to everyone thus its long-term popularity! Sing the song without the harmonica and listen for which notes are where. It is fine to look at the sheet music and learn it, but that may be a big step for a beginner. Until you decide to take that leap just focus on listening to the note lengths.

```
6   5    5    5         5    5    5
Oh  Jin-gle bells,  Jin-gle bells

5    6    4    -4   5
Jin-gle  all  the  way

-5  -5   -5   -5  5   5   5
Oh  what fun  it  is  to  ride

5   5 5    -4       -4 5    -4   6
in  a one  horse  o-pen  slei-gh
```

Beethoven's "Ode to Joy" is another well-known tune because of its memorable and brilliant simplicity. It is mostly quarter notes, but it also includes an eighth note right before the music resolves. This is a key feature of compositions that we will see repeatedly, good ones have a peak and resolution of the music. Keep in mind "Ode to Joy" normally has no lyrics so you just have to play the riff below. Can you spot (or hear!) where the 1/8 note is? If not it is the second to last draw 4 note.

```
5  5  -5  6  6  -5  5  -4  4  4  -4  5  5  -4  -4
```

If you do not like classical or traditional, that is fine as popular music uses these same beat principles. The bass often uses quarter notes as it "walks" the listener along the rhythm. Rock and Roll loves hi-hat eighth hits and funk is funky because it uses sixteenth notes in its groove. When we further break the beat up, we can use syncopation and swing to make people want to shake their butts and dance about! Remember that syncopation is stressing offbeats while swing is where the music is spaced a little bit, with swing we play certain parts off time. A listening example will be the best way to hear the difference.

🔊

11. Syncopation vs Swing

Popular Harmonica Rhythms

As you work on getting your single notes down you can start practicing rhythms you hear or read. Thanks to the harmonica's vocal nature we can find a lot of potential rhythms and soundbites with our mouths. Listen to a song you like and start using your mouth and tongue to make the rhythm, it sounds silly but play drums with your mouth. Tap your tongue inside to the cymbals and then make a pucker to copy the bass drum sound with an "ooh." Move back and forth to the beat like an early hominid just discovering music! Now do that same thing with a harmonica in your mouth, play the beat through it.

🔊

12. Harmonica Rhythms

Count along with the music and be sure to add rests in, sometimes it is the lack of the beat that can add tension and resolution into a song. A rest can create anticipation in the right context and most of all it allows you to breathe. When playing any breathing instrument, it is always important to breathe at the right time! When you're in the middle of a driving rhythm it can be hard to find the right time to take a breath. Such a beat is like the train groove or the chug, to make that you will again copy the sound of a train like a kid and then play it! When the groove propels the song along, we have to get clever in how we breathe. One simple way is to add draw notes in allowing you a moment!

We haven't looked at blues playing yet because you still need to learn to bend but this basic blues rhythm can be done with straight harp. This riff can be played by starting on a 4(B) moving to a 5 (D), then 5(B) and finally ending on the 4(B) again. If you are sloppy in this it still sounds bluesy and cool but at this point it is imperative to try for single notes.

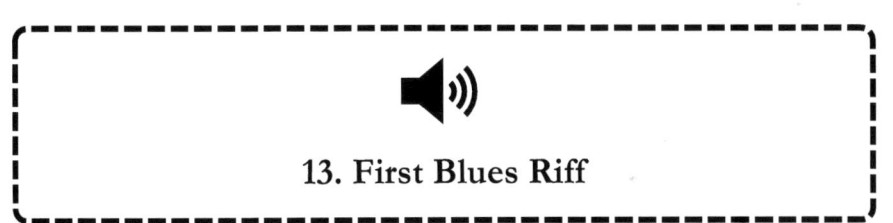

🔊

13. First Blues Riff

Remember

- The beats are just as important as the notes if we want the song to sound right. If we do not play the notes for the correct time the piece will not work.

- You don't need sheet music to learn rhythm, it's all about listening to songs and copying the groove. Sing the rhythm and then play it into the harp.

- Syncopation and swing will be important in your harmonica playing as accenting or changing the timing of the beat will give your music more emotion and drive.

Trivia

- One of the greatest drummers and masters of the beat was Buddy Rich and he had strong opinions of practice. Instead of sitting alone and repeating technique it was more important to go play with other musicians.

- Many genres with syncopation derived from groups who did hard labor like African slaves, immigrants, and physical laborers. Syncopation is helpful to keep a large group of people together during work.

- Your brain deals with rhythm in the cerebellum, as opposed to the auditory cortex where you process pitch. That's a great groove that can reach the deepest recesses of our minds!

Chapter 5

A Closer Look At Notes

Topics Covered

- Music Note Theory

- What Are Intervals, Scales, and Chords

- Diatonic Vs Chromatic

- Note distances give us emotion

Just as the beat can give a specific vibe so do notes! Often people fear this aspect of music theory, but it is far easier than most realize. There are only 12 notes and once you know the basic patterns it will open up a world of understanding. A piano keyboard or digital app will be really helpful to see how simple these 12 notes can be.

Notes and Their Intervals

We often suggest students play in the key of C because that has no sharps or flats and is easier to process. The long (often white) keys on a piano are the natural and the short (often black) keys can be the sharps or flats depending upon how we are naming the scale. If we just play all the long keys, it will sound good as that is the C major scale. Your diatonic harmonica has only the major scale, so it is hard to play a wrong note in that key. Let's take a step back from the diatonic and look at all 12 notes of the chromatic scale.

C C#/Db D D#/Eb E F F#/Gb G G#/Ab A A#/Bb B C

The notes that have two names are enharmonic like C# is enharmonic with Db, the composer chooses which they will use. Each note is exactly one key apart on a keyboard and that is called a semitone or half-step movement, all 12 notes are one semitone apart. Notice that there is no short key between E and F nor B and C, they are also a half step apart. These spaces between the intervals and how they sound are essential to the overall vibe of our music. If we play the notes C to C# it can be menacing or sad, they are known as a minor interval, the stronger intervals are major, and the strongest intervals are called perfect. You may recognize the C-F# as the tritone or the devil's interval because it has such a dissonant sound.

14. Intervals

These minor, major, and perfect intervals are mixed in songs to create emotions and feelings. When a songwriter is hired to write a tune or jingle they do not just grasp ideas out of thin air, they us specific intervals to create an experience in the listener. The next step after intervals is putting them together to form scales, you already know the major (or diatonic) and chromatic. When we play the chromatic there are all the same half step intervals so that doesn't work as a song, there is no defined tonal point. However, when we start picking specific notes and putting them together, we get more distinct sounds. To find any major scale we start at any note on the keyboard and use (w)whole steps and (h)half steps like

A Closer Look At Notes

this W-W-H-W-W-W-H. If you start at the C note and apply that pattern you will get C-D-E-F-G-A-B and back to C again!. Any root note that you start on this pattern will give you its major scale.

Now once we know what the major scale is we label it with numbers as 1 2 3 4 5 6 7 and from here all other scales can be labeled as compared to the major. For example, the minor scale is 1 2 b3 4 5 b6 b7 this means that the 3, 6, 7 degrees are flat, so a C minor scale is C D Eb F G Ab Bb. Now in the minor scale we have more minor intervals so of course our overall vibe will be sad and melancholy. Our blues scale formula is 1 b3 4 b5 5 b7 which means we have minor and tritone intervals in their which is why the blues sound so sad and dissonant. Basically, you can look at your intervals as flavor, if you play perfect notes, you have strong and positive simple songs. Once you start adding in minors, majors, and tritones our music gets richer and can tug on our emotions more. You will not be able to play the minor or blues scale yet as you need to learn to bend, but it is still essential to grasp how your notes relate.

Another popular scale, which we can play now, is the pentatonic, its formula is 1 2 3 5 6, so it is missing the 4 and 7. The pentatonic scale is one of the most universal features among all people on Earth. If an alien species landed the most powerful and agreed upon response would likely be that scale as it is ever present. And because the scale degrees of 4 and 7 are missing it fits with almost anything. To play this scale on the harmonica we use 4(B) 4(D) 5(B) 6(B) 6(D) 7(B). Many musicians use pentatonic scales to solo as they are safe notes, their intervals and spacing are all consonant. However, they can also create pretty boring music, beloved yes, but without some more dissonant flavor it may not be interesting. Just as we want an on beat and offbeat we also need a mix of consonance and dissonance to make a great song.

Next, we can start stacking our notes in the scale to get chords, by mixing the 1-3-5 scale degrees we get a major chord. On your harmonica if you blow more than three holes at once you are playing the 1-3-5 notes (in the key of C that's C-E-G). When we make a minor chord, we use 1-b3-5 (or C-Eb-G) and while this may seem complicated remember that the underlying intervals still work. You can also flatten or raise the 5th to get a diminished or augmented sound in your chord, of course because you introduce dissonant intervals. As a single note melody instrument, you will not be playing many chords on the diatonic harmonica, but you will be adding notes to the chords the band plays. It will be up to you to know what kind of scale and vibe you are going to use to fit in.

After we build chords, we then turn them into chord progressions which may seem like a huge jump but it's not. Our chord progressions carry over the same feelings! If they are built on perfect and major intervals the song is strong and dominating, if it has minor and tritones it will be sad, lonely, or maybe just bluesy. Music is not rocket science, there are 12 notes that can be stacked and played in different patterns and that's it!

Applying Music Theory to Harmonica

It might seem silly to look at all the notes on a piano when the harmonica only has a diatonic scale, but we need to see the bigger picture before we can get more out of our instrument. Now you

A Closer Look At Notes

hopefully realize why you can't just pick up a regular harmonica and play any song. A chromatic harmonica however has a little plate attached to a button that opens new holes up for the rest of the notes that we lack on the diatonic. In the meantime, we will focus more on the theory of our simple diatonic harp. We know the blow notes are all from the major chord but what about when we draw? Let's take a look at the C major harmonica notes one more time.

C	E	G	C	E	G	C	E	G	C
1	2	3	4	5	6	7	8	9	10
D	G	B	D	F	A	B	D	F	A

When we draw on holes 2-3-4, we get the notes G-B-D which make a G major chord. Let's check to make sure, start on the root G and use the W-W-H-W-W-W-H and we will get G-A-B-C-D-E-F#-G and so the major chord is G-B-D. In fact, most of those draw notes fit the G major scale except for the F, it is flat and not sharp. Notice in the G major scale a flat F is a b7 degree, which is essential for the blues. That is why harmonicas are so suited to the blues, the draw notes allow you to play some *blue* or flattened notes! So far, our playing has been in the first position but when we focus on the draw notes it is called second position. Often in blues we play a harp in its second position so if the song is in G, we play a C harp in second position. If you are playing another key besides C, draw on the 2 hole and that note will be the second position key.

15. First and Second Position

Since you know your major and minor scale formula, we can find another chord on this harmonica by drawing at the 8-9-10, be gentle so it doesn't screech. If you do it right you hit the notes D-F-A, let's do some reverse engineering to find what chord that is. The D major scale is D E F# G A B C# and the major chord is D-F#-A. So, if we flatten that F, we get a Dm. So, if we blow anywhere, we get a C major, drawing at 2-3-4 is a G major and the 8-9-10 draw is a Dm. While we don't often play chords on the harmonica, having these as references can help navigate the holes.

If you do not have a key of C harmonica that's ok as all of this info is still relative, you are just in a different key. If you try to jam with a backing track and the key is not the same, it will sound off. One great exercise to train your ears is to play a long white key on the keyboard and then find the right harmonica hole that matches. This is tedious and hard for beginners but there is no better exercise to get to know your notes. It's also imperative to start actively listening to all the music that you like and identifying the potential notes being used. Besides applying our theory to the harmonica, we need to look and listen to the bigger picture, so all of this info starts to click.

Folk and traditional music will often use major or minor keys with simple and consonant intervals, usually pentatonic scales. Heavy metal likes power chords made up of the 1 and 5 scale degrees along with minor chords over it. Blues rock often has a major bed of music peppered with blue and minor notes. While jazz and soul love to extend their chords. A jazz chord may be a C7b5 or even a C13, which may seem mind blowing but it's just a matter of stacking more notes from the next octave. The more complicated the music the more chord extensions and note intervals will be used. Genres like progressive rock and fusion will also have tough scales and chords. However, to be clear, more notes doesn't make the music better, that is all about personal preference!

This is why we start beginners on simple genres, as long as you play the right key with a pentatonic scale it's hard to make a mistake. Once you add in more chords and intervals our notes we can choose narrow and we have more chance of messing up. Guitar solo shredders will often use the major or minor pentatonic, so they sound better, the same goes for harmonica, it helps to play the safe notes. Once the player gets the basics down, they can start dipping into jazz and improvisation. During this chapter we have discussed some notes that may not seem possible on the diatonic. In reality there are more notes available, you just have to bend by moving your tongue, next we will take a look at ways to get more notes out of the blow and draw.

At this point your practicing should start getting more refined and be broken up into sections. Everyday practice the major scale up and down and in different beat patterns like a mixture of quarter and eighth notes. Refine playing your G major and D minor shapes and play each individual note. This is a good point to also start playing along with backing tracks, improvise both on the low chords, middle melody, and high-pitched wails for embellishment.

Remember

- Try not to mix up different formula and pattern naming systems. When we say a major chord is made up of scale degrees 1, 3, and 5 that is not the same as holes blown.

- Music theory has many approaches and methods even the most educated musicians will argue over similar concepts.

- The notes and intervals you use will ultimately provide the emotional context for the listener, so choose wisely!

Trivia

- The common modes that often confuse students are simply different orders of the major scale. However, the intervals change which makes the modes unique from each other.

- Music theory is more than just your pitch names, it also describes the harmony, rhythm, and all musical aspects. By actively studying all parts of the songs you like it will increase your knowledge of the topic.

- Western music works in semitones, if you care to study quarter tones or microtonal music there are many other cultures that break their notes up further than halves.

Chapter 6

Crossharp

Topics Covered

- The difference between straight and cross harp

- How to bend notes

- How to overblow notes

In this chapter we are going to look at some harmonica techniques that will potentially be harder than you expect. These concepts can take time (sometimes months to years) so don't worry if you don't have it by the end of the chapter. You are likely still struggling with single notes, but it doesn't hurt to expand in your harmonica practice. Now that you are aware of a little music theory on notes the concepts of changing the pitch should be a little easier. All you have to do is work daily at it!

What Is Crossharp?

We played a little 1-4 interval blues riff earlier, but it wasn't the same as a true blues harp sound. If your goal is to wail on the harmonica and jam, then you will need to learn crossharp or the second position. To recap when we draw the 2-3-4, we get a G chord, if we start on the 2 Draw that is the G note and where the second position begins. Crossharp is simply focusing on that G major scale instead of blowing the C major. If we start at a G root and apply W-W-H-W-W-W-H we get G A B C D E F# G.

C	E	G	C	E	G	C	E	G	C
1	2	3	4	5	6	7	8	9	10
D	G	B	D	F	A	B	D	F	A

You may notice that the G major scale is not easy to find in a straight order like the first position, and there is no F sharp! But the scale is there, and we get it by manipulating the air over the reeds to find new notes. The initial hurdle you will face in playing in second position is that the focus is on drawing air in. We will at times still be blowing as some blow notes fit the G major scale, but too much and the tonal center moves back to C major. The main reason this position is so perfect for blues and rock is that drawing air in makes a much cooler "wail." When we play crosssharp correctly the harmonica will sound soulful with more of a vocal nature.

Another reason that position works well for blues is that it gives you a mode that works great for the genre. The diatonic modes are scales that derive from the major scale with the formula 1 2 3 4 5 6 7. If we flatten the 7th, we will be in a famous mode for rock known as Mixolydian. Go back to the G major scale and flatten the 7th, G Mixolydian is G A B C D E F G which suits the notes above better! Take a look at your piano or keyboard app and play both the G major scale (Ionian mode) and G Mixolydian, notice how that one change in the F makes a difference in the overall feel. When you flatten that 7th interval it suddenly has a minor vibe which along with a strong backbeat is a feature of rock!

If a guitarist is playing a blues tune in G you will use 2nd position of your C harp and this will allow you to play in G with them. There is also a third position to play in, for that we start on the 4 draw or the note D. Of course, if that is our root we have a new scale in D. Go back to the W-W-H-W-W-W-H formula to get the scale D E F# G A B C# D. We don't see any F# and C# so it's clearly not the D major scale, the notes we do have are D E F G A B C D or 1 2 b3 4 5 6 b7. This is known as Dorian mode and features the b3 and b7, if you play it on your keyboard, it is a slightly more minor and sad sound than Mixolydian. Dorian mode songs are often sad, dramatic, or even funky at times because they rely more minor chords. When we decide we have to play in another harmonica position it is important to play the right root and only keep to safe notes.

When we play major or Ionian music there is a focus on the middle part of the harp and mostly easy blow notes. However, when we dip into the 2nd and 3rd positions for blues then it is important to focus on draws and bends as a way to manipulate your notes. Not only does that technique help play more notes it also gives us the wailing sounds that are common in blues and rock. Just be prepared as bending is one of the hardest things for a new harmonica player to do!

Bend The Note!

It turns out that you can play more notes than you see in the blows and draws by changing the air flow in your mouth and body cavity. If you angle your tongue up to the roof of the mouth and nearly cut the air off, you "bend" the note. You may have already discovered this when moving your tongue around in various manners, perhaps the note has wavered a little. One of the reasons it is so hard for beginners to grasp the concept is because it is so difficult to describe the exact motion of the tongue in the mouth. It's often portrayed as forming a "k" sound but that isn't quite what is happening. It's more accurate to say the shape of the tongue right before you make the "k" will give you a bend. And it's not just about the shape of the tongue, it also matters how the air passes across it.

If you can whistle it may help you learn the process of bending better, whistle the theme to Happy Birthday slowly and pay attention to how the air passes through. As you change notes your tongue is slightly moving, and the air pressure changes to allow for a new pitch. This similar concept is what we are doing with our harmonica, by making slight changes in our mouth we can get new notes out of some of the reeds. Besides whistling another method to find your bend is to say the word "we" as you draw air in, it will feel strange, now change the word to "ew". Notice how the air passing over your tongue changes when you do this into the 4 draw it should start giving you the bend sound. There are other holes to bend but master that 4 first.

If you are still struggling with clean notes, then it will be almost impossible to get a bend. Once you try to bend from more than one hole it's a cacophony of noise. One of the best ways to work on your bends is to start learning the blues scale which has the formula 1 b3 4 b5 5 b7. Before we find that on the harp let's break down why it is called the blues scale. The blue notes are the b3, b5, and b7 and they are all present in the blues scale. If we use G as our root that will give us the notes G Bb C Db D F G.

Crossharp

The notes G, C, D, and F are accessible but what about the Bb and Db, those we get by bending! Start on the draw 2 at the G and next we move to a bend on 3 to get Bb. Change your mouth shape to play the Bb instead of a B. Next is C on the 4 blow which is easy but after we have to draw and bend our 4 to get a Db before we can play the draw 4 of D. Then we do a regular draw on hole 5 for F and end on a 6 blow with G. This will not be easy at first, don't draw too hard on the 2 and 3 as playing louder doesn't help. Now that we are doing bends we need a new method in our harmonica tabs, we can use a slash / to indicate a draw bend. This will give us a blues harmonica scale with this tab.

-2 -3/ 4 -4/ -4 -5 6 (ascending G Bb C Db D F G)

6 -5 -4 -4/ 4 -3/ -2 (descending G F D Db C Bb G)

🔊

16. G Blues Scale Bend

Normally when we play a blues scale, we go to the top at 6 and then repeat the -5 again before descending like in the recording. It may help to only play the scale going down it as it may be easier to go from the 4 draw to the 4 bend rather than the other way around. Take each note slowly and make sure they sound right compared to the scale on a keyboard. Visualize hitting the pitch in your mouth that you can hear. This may sound silly but remember that this is a vocal instrument, and an extension of your voice. When you sing or whistle another pitch you are imagining it in your head before you do it. Copy this same process onto the harmonica. You can also bend other holes and when you do the note decreases by a semitone. So if you bend the hole 1 you get Db like hole 4 and a hole 2 bend will be F#.

Overblows and Overdraws

Just as we can change our mouth and air on a draw, we can also do it while blowing and it is known as an overblow. To be clear though this doesn't mean you blow air in a hard manner once again it is just changing the pitch. When we overblow (or overdraw) we are usually jumping more than a half step hence the word "over," it has more to do with our notes than our air pressure. To overblow we will go from the regular pucker and single note blow to shaping our mouth by saying "he" into the harp. Like the bend this changes the air and we should get a new sound. If we overblow at whole 5, we will get an F#, so we jump from a regular E note on the blow to that. Sometimes students will struggle with these, other times if you have the bend down it may be easier. Even if you can't do either at this point it is ok as long as you understand what we are doing.

Now we can look at how to play a 2nd position major scale as some new notes have opened up! Remember we are in G major in 2nd position on the C harp and we need the notes G A B C D E F# G. The start is clearly on the draw 2 with G but where can we get the A? Well, we have to bend the 3 even more, it has to be lowered from Bb to A. The notes B C D E are easy but now to get that F# we have to overblow on the 5 and it finishes back on the G at the 6 blow. Here is the second position major scale formula where a double slash // equals a whole step bend and a * equals an overblow.

-2 -3// -3 4 -4 5 5* 6

Crossharp

17. Overblow

Don't expect that the whole step bend to be easy, you will struggle and as always that is normal. Hopefully though you are starting to see these patterns and focal points on the harp and most of all it is important to get to know tabs. If you want to learn sheet music that is fine but as a beginner focus on being able to read and understand tabs and scales. If you struggle with the full major or blues scale you can play safe notes in the major and minor pentatonic. The minor is a lot better than the major which is another reason why the 2nd position blues are so popular, it is easier!

Major Pentatonic -2 -3// -3 -4 5 6

Minor Pentatonic -2 -3/ 4 -4 -5 6

18. Reality of Bends and Overblows

A human voice sings the blues thanks to melisma or the smooth run of note intervals. When you hear an R&B artist sing, they are soulful because they blend blue notes into their vocal run. As a harmonicist that will be your same goal to wail, bend, and overblow your notes to turn them into something more. Just like those singers they didn't learn this overnight it took months and years of practice.

You can stick with major scales and traditional songs and be a great player but if you want to play harmonica that will get attention it helps to bend and play second position crossharp style.

Remember

- Do not over wiggle your tongue just make smooth movements to find the right bend spot

- Do not blow or draw harder to bend or overblow, more air is not the key. You need the proper air and space.

- Hollow out your mouth and throat when altering notes and arch your tongue when necessary.

- Don't spend too long on this practice, put in little bits into your daily practice, any obsession or excess time usually doesn't help. Be steady and patient!

Trivia

- When you hear the harmonica in most blues and rock songs it is likely on 2nd position. Folk and country however will often be played straight with more blowing.

- On a C harmonica hole 3 can be bent to Ab and hole 10 can be overblown to Bb which is a huge jump. Don't expect to be able to do this for a while though.

- There are many great harmonica players but one of the best to listen to for bends is Little Walter out of Chicago.

Chapter 7

Harmonica Techniques

Topics Covered

- Tongue Blocking

- Dynamics

- Vibrato and Tremolo

- Different varieties of harmonica

There is still more music theory and rhythms to learn but for now you have a solid foundation to build on. As we try new techniques keep working on your scales, songs, clean notes, and bends. If you still struggle just keep working at it. In the meantime, we will look at some basic tips and tricks to make your harmonica sound better. Some of these concepts you may have already discovered if you are experimenting but let's take a closer look.

Tongue Blocking

Our focus on single notes has been all based around the pucker but we can also tongue block. This is exactly how it sounds where we use the tongue to block the holes we don't want to play. As we learn this technique, we can use our first songs and scales again and focus on the new way to play them. Start by putting your mouth over holes 1-4 all at once and blow now push your tongue against the holes 1-3 until you hear a clean sound coming from 4. If you smash the tongue tip into hole 1 the rest of it should cover 1, 2, and 3. As always don't blow too hard to get the right sound, it will take time to find the right position, a lot of experimenting with listening for the right note. The next step is to play your major scale with tongue blocking. Block 1, 2, and 3 and then blow and draw 4, next move over and do hole 5 and then 6 before ending on 7. Remember the hole 7 has a draw then blow in the major scale!

This will be tedious to learn, and you may wonder what is the point if you can do the pucker? You can play blues riffs faster with a tongue block rather than a pucker as there is less movement of the harmonica. It may feel like you are starting the learning process over again, but it will only reinforce your scale and playing knowledge. There are also other techniques to practice along with the tongue blocking. You can slap the holes with your tongue to create a staccato or driving sound or you can sweep your tongue across the right notes. If you move the tongue fast you can also create a fluttering sound. Eventually you will mix both puckering and tongue blocking depending on which is the best fit for the song.

U blocking is a tongue technique where you make the shape of a U and then block the holes on each side of where you are blowing. Not everyone can do this as sometimes people cannot make that shape so don't push yourself if it is a struggle. To start you will approach the holes as if you are doing the pucker and aim for hole 4. Instead, if using the pucker though you will form that U shape and block holes 3 and 5. One of the main advantages of this odd tongue movement is on the high notes where many struggle. As of now you are still a beginner at harmonica so keep this technique in the back of your mind to occasionally approach.

Just be careful and don't injure your tongue by trying to move it in a way you can't. Like all other harmonica techniques, they seem impossible at first but after a few months of steady work they start to get better.

The best players use a variety of embouchures depending on what sounds and works best for them. You may find some songs work better with tongue blocking or pucker, practice them both as they will help expand your style and train your mouth better. The ultimate goal is to learn how best to articulate the right sounds. Remember in earlier chapters where we were forming the letter t and k, those were examples of articulation. The wider musical concept of articulation is how a single note sounds and that can be changed with more than the tongue. You can change the pitch and dynamics of a note with your angle of play, pucker, blocking, and many more mouth movements. Since playing the harmonica is an extension of our voice, we can articulate notes in any way we see fit to get a desired sound. You can even invent your own methods to get a specific sound, listen to the music you hear and try to copy it with any mouth movement possible. Sometimes when learning a new technique, a player may even stumble onto a new skill. Always keep track of your embouchure to produce the best sounds you can.

Vibrato, Tremolo, and Shakes

Tremolo is the change in volume and vibrato is the change in pitch. If you have an electric guitar with a tremolo bar you may notice that it was misnamed, technically when you bend the whammy bar it changes the pitch. Because of this mistake back in the 50's many people sometimes confuse these concepts. There are different methods for getting these techniques on the harmonica. Sometimes when we cup our hand our vibrate our throat it is possible to get both techniques at the same time so make sure you are hearing the difference.

If you go back to the hand flutter near the beginning of the book that was an example of tremolo as the volume is going up and down depending on if the hand is open or closed. Usually when it involves a hand movement it will be changing the volume, so how do we alter the pitch to get vibrato? That can be done with the tongue like bending or it can also be accomplished in the back of the throat. Imagine singing vibrato with your voice, to get that effect we have to vibrate our vocal cords. This may be difficult at first on the harmonica and if so, try moving your tongue around like when you bend the note, except faster. Listen for a change in the pitch and not just the volume to get a proper sound.

Initially most of the vibrato you do will be in your mouth like when you are bending a note. However, as you progress start focusing that pitch alteration at the back of the mouth and into the throat. Draw notes will be the best to practice vibrato on and it will sound weird at first and likely be more of a tremolo. You may still struggle to do it as you are likely pulling to hard and running out of breath. With practice it should get a little easier to differentiate between a pitch or volume change. Like the bend itself there is no magic approach that will make it simple, it just requires listening, copying, and understanding what is happening to the note.

As you get these concepts down it will be possible to do things like trills, warbles, and shakes. These are all essential parts of blues harp and what make those players sound so cool. Just remember that as a beginner it will not be easy to jump into those techniques. If you are playing on a daily basis and adjusting your embouchure and throat muscles they will start to appear and when they do, repeat the process. Of course, don't forget to use your hands to shake or change the overall sound. Even though you are playing a diatonic harmonica it is possible to pull all sorts of notes and vibes out of it if you focus on mouth, tongue, and hand movement.

> 🔊
>
> **19. Tremolo and Vibrato**

Playing Other Styles of Harmonica

You may not be that interested in blues harmonica, which is fine as there are plenty of other styles to play. After a while playing straight harp simple songs may get boring, if you have mastered single note playing you may be ready to play a chromatic harmonica. They are more expensive but many of the same concepts we have learned here still apply. The main difference is now you have a button that will block the holes and create new ones which allows you to play more notes with no bending. It can get very confusing fast though when you first start playing chromatic as you need to remember whether you are blowing or drawing with the button open or closed. If you have a chromatic harmonica, you really don't need another guide to play, just compare notes to the piano and listen. Remember ear training is the best practice ever!

The tremolo harmonica is similar to a diatonic except the notes are doubled up to create a fuller sound. The tuning on these doubled up notes isn't perfect though; the reeds are slightly out of tune, so they end up having a tremolo effect. It can create a beat or flutter effect without shaking or altering your hand or mouth. Tremolo harmonicas are common in Celtic and Asian folk music if you prefer those genres. Octave harmonicas also use two holes as opposed to one on the diatonic but instead of being slightly off tune they are pitched an octave apart. This spacing creates a much fuller sound with an almost chorus vibe where more than one harmonica is playing. If you have really developed a love for this instrument, it is great to buy different styles.

It won't hurt your diatonic playing if you expand into different models. In fact, picking up any other instrument is just going to expand your greater knowledge of music. If you are hitting a wall with single note playing, bending, and other techniques you can always add other instruments in to sound better. Bob Dylan is not an amazing harmonica player, but when he adds his basic riffs with his vocals and guitar it sounds great. Don't stress about getting every single technique down perfectly, just play music. If you want to jam on blues, try the diatonic or if you prefer jazz the chromatic will be more helpful. Either way the main goal is to play whatever music you can, and if you keep at it those unattainable skills and techniques will suddenly be possible.

Troubleshooting

At this point you know how to read tabs, understand some basic music theory, and you should be getting good at playing along to a beat or backing track. If the actual harmonica playing and techniques are still giving you trouble it may help to troubleshoot your problems. The first step is to pinpoint the issue and then research through books or online sites. One of the best skills a musician can have is searching online or on social media for an answer!

The first thing to remember about any problems you have is that it is usually your technique, not the harmonica. Sometimes broken, bent, or jammed reeds occur, maybe some food particles got stuck. If you feel the reeds are off you can open it up and check them. Or if you are certain your harmonica has an issue, try getting a new one! If the issue persists it is definitely your playing that is the problem. As long as you can play simple beginning songs then it likely works fine. If your issue is with bending and vibrato then you simply need to practice more. Many players do not like to admit that they simply aren't good enough yet and that can be detrimental. You want to stay positive, and goal oriented in practice, but you also need to admit when you are struggling.

One great way to troubleshoot your issues is to try different teaching methods and teachers, not everyone has the same luck with the same lessons. There is always another approach to different techniques, even if practice is going well it can't hurt to try new methods. Social media groups and forums are also a great place to ask others about your progress and where you may receive help. Just be careful as these places can also break your spirit with rude attitudes from those who know how to play. It's important as a musician to grow some thick skin and ignore comments that are not helpful.

And the final and best way to troubleshoot your problems is to play with other musicians. Join a band, form a band, or go to a jam session and watch others play. When you feel comfortable play along and see how you do. Let go of worries about impressing people and just play what you want. After reading this book you already have a decent idea of some music theory so you will be ahead of most musicians. By playing with others, it will force you to fit in and actively listen, which will improve your playing. Play simple riffs at first and with each practice try something new. If you absolutely have no band to play with you can use a DAW like Logic or Pro Tools to record yourself as a band. Make your own songs with backing tracks and try new techniques.

In this next chapter we will focus on how to play both straight and cross harp along with backing tracks. If you play guitar, ukulele, or piano you can buy a metal harmonica neck holder and use that to play both the harp and other instruments. Just be sure whether you are in first or second position and that your key matches what you're playing.

Remember

- Vibrato and tremolo are often confused, just be sure to listen to tell if the note has a beat and volume change or if the actual pitch itself is changing.

- Even if you like the pucker it is important to learn the tongue blocking as well, both techniques are essential.

- The best way to get better at harmonica techniques is to play with a band or multi-tracking DAW software. Play many songs, genres, and meters to grasp the larger picture.

Trivia

- Some of the most well-known pop harmonica players are not musically that great at it, they just use the instrument as a filler like John Lennon on "Love Me Do."

- As we said in the beginning, the harmonica is often associated with folk and simple blues. While wailing and bending is incredible most people play simple songs and ditties.

- This instrument is completely self-contained and set up for a player with no lessons or musical skills. While lessons and advanced techniques are great, the harmonica can be played by anyone on their own if they just practice often. You don't need a teacher for great skill at it!

Chapter 8

Jamming With Your Harmonica

Topics Covered

- Finding the key to backing music

- Which position to pick

- How to jam

- Backing tracks

How To Jam

The first step to jamming is finding other band members or music to play with. Since we cannot guarantee you can find others, we can use modern technology or even music on the radio. The easiest way to improvise or jam along is to find backing drum tracks and drum machines. DAWs like Logic, Pro Tools, and even electronic dance music ones like Ableton will allow you to easily create a backing drum track. There are also apps for phones and tablets that are funk, rock, Latin, metal, and many other genres. Download these apps, turn a groove on and just start playing!

Remember music is all about tension and release or consonance and dissonance. We start on a root note like the draw 4 and go up the scale to build tension, maybe move into the higher notes to create more. Then when we feel, the musical phrase is coming to an end we can end on a lower full chord. Most songs are in 8 or 12 bars so our phrases will usually be those amounts. Modern songs are also often broken down as intro, verse, chorus, bridge or solo, and finally an outro. The verses and choruses repeat so keep the same musical phrase for each of those sections. Look up the music that you like best and break it down into its different sections. If you struggle at first playing notes in your jam, just focus on matching the rhythm and beat.

The harder part is jamming with more than drums, once bass, guitar, or piano is added in we have to make sure the key is the same. If you are making music yourself in an app or DAW, you can control the key you pick. Otherwise, if you want to jam to famous music or full backing tracks you have to find the key. You can look up the key or simply play along and see what fits. The piano or keyboard app will allow you to play notes and see what fits. Again, this process is tedious but great for ear training. If you just have a C harmonica then you will need to stick to first position C and second position G. Luckily many popular songs are in one of those keys!

> 🔊
>
> **20. Backing Track 2 Rock Jam No Key**

One thing to be careful of is that songs can be slowed down or sped up which will change their key and sometimes musicians simply change keys to give a different vibe in the song. If you are playing along and it sounds great and suddenly it doesn't then the song may have changed key. Here is a simple lone drum track along with a country or folk backing track to play some C first position over.

> 🔊
> **21. Backing Track 4 Country Folk First Position**

The easiest songs to jam with will be traditional or pop tunes that are in one key and have no blue notes. But many harmonica players do not want to play that, they want the blues! In that case you will find keys more suited to second position playing. Be sure to start on the draw 2 note and keep the tonal center where it belongs. As you play along don't constrict yourself and be rigid, this is the blues or rock, and you need to loosen up and emote! There is no right or wrong way to jam or improvise, the key is just play and listen for what sounds good.

> 🔊
> **22. Backing Track 3 Funky Second Position**

> 🔊
> **23. Backing Track 5 12 Bar Blues 2nd Position**

Eventually you will want to get other diatonic keys so you have more options in what music you can play along with. Most of all it really helps to find others to play with. You can try social media like TikTok that allows you to duet other videos, when you hear someone playing an instrument see if you can add something to it. Those who succeed at music will just jump right in and do it, it's ok to be afraid but nothing serious will happen if you mess up. The more you engage with songs, musicians, and play your harmonica the more the techniques and theory in this book will start to click and you will be on your way to being a great improviser!

Amplifiers, Mics, and Other Gear

If you have a guitar or ukulele buy a metal harmonica holder so you can play along with it. Pick a chord progression that will go well with your C harmonica, perhaps the chords C-F-G. Play these and add in harmonica during the intros and bridge/solo. It will be a noticeable difference when playing with it in your hands or in the holder, it takes some getting used to! The more you add harmonica to other instruments successfully the better you will get at your theory and overall understanding.

Once you start to get some confidence in your playing you may want to buy gear to join a band or play live shows. We aren't going to name specific brands here but there are microphones made just for harmonicas and they are the best. Whether you use one of them or a regular mic keep in mind you will be blowing right into it, so the power and levels need to be watched. The best kinds of amplifiers are those with cleaner sounds, crunch is more for metal while clean is for blues and pop. Just remember if you decide to play into a mic and amp any mistakes you make will be much louder so practice as much as possible before using them.

If you really fall in love with the harmonica then it is fine to buy more keys, a mic, amp, and even a mixer and DAW to record yourself. However, the beauty of the harmonica is its simplicity and portability. By itself you can take it anywhere and always be ready to play a simple ditty or song. And if you do find some other musicians to play with, just make sure they are in the right key!

Chapter 9

Deep Cleaning, Repair, and Conclusion

Topics Covered

- Deep cleaning the insides of the harmonica

- Broken combs

- When to repair and when to pay someone

Deep Cleaning Your Harmonica

As you have been playing you should be knocking the saliva and gunk out of your harmonica but eventually it will need a deeper cleaning. For this process all you need is rubbing alcohol, vinegar, and some light brushes, perhaps a paint or toothbrush. The main thing to focus on is using light amounts of chemicals and no hard scrubbing.

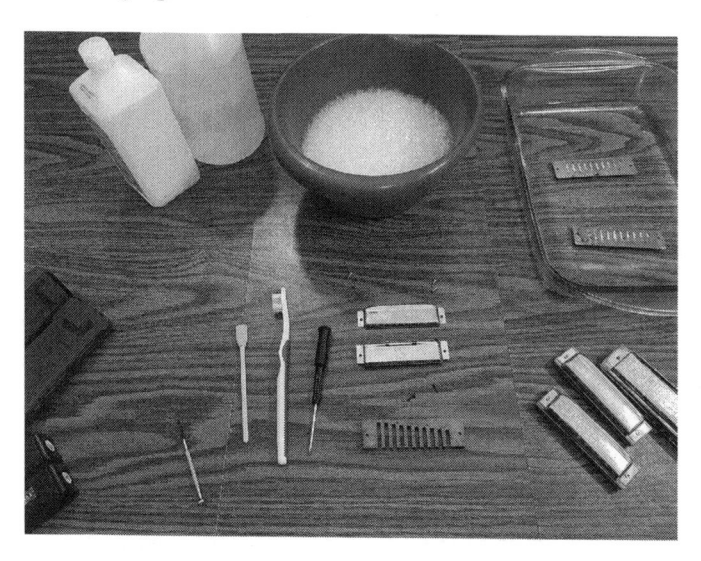

As you take the harmonica apart make sure you have a clean space and plenty of room. Take pictures if necessary and keep all the parts lined up so you don't question where it all went as you put it back together. The comb can be cleaned with dish detergent and water, don't soak it just give it a light brushing. If it is wood and it gets too wet, it will need a long time to dry out. Scrub it lightly and remove any foreign particles. The brass reeds can be soaked in a mix of water about 10 parts added to 1 part vinegar. Sometimes people add lemon juice instead, a light acidic solution will help clear any spots or residue. If you must brush the reeds do it as gently as possible or the bristles will catch them and bend or break it off.

The top and bottom plates can be cleaned with a cloth and some rubbing alcohol. If there are any repairs needed now is the time to do them. Sometimes the comb reeds break, these can be glued back into place with the tiniest amount of glue (notice in the photo below the third longest comb is bent). Broken reeds can be unscrewed and replaced with new ones ordered online. The cost of the repair should be weighed with what kind of harmonica you have. If it's a cheaper one it may be better to just get a new harp. However, if the instrument is a pro model and very expensive it is best to let a more experienced person handle it.

Deep Cleaning, Repair, and Conclusion

It is possible to find deals online if you buy used harps, and deep cleaning them is a great experience. If you want to have all 12 keys for the first and second position, then that is the most affordable way to do it. Or if you want to dive into different harmonicas like the chromatic, octave, or tremolo used ones are a great way to save money and see if they work for you. The good news is that like playing a harmonica, cleaning and repairing them is also easy for most people. It truly is one of the most accessible instruments.

Conclusion

There you have most of the techniques and basic music theory needed to play the harmonica. If you have learned a lot and it is going well, just keep at it. Stopping will make it so you may lose any progress, practice should always be a daily thing if you want to excel and jam or improvise. If you haven't learned much and are still struggling, that's ok and common. Most people fail at music many times before one day it will just click. This is not the greatest news to those having trouble, but it is the truth! Whether you want to play guitar, piano, banjo, violin, or maybe sing they all take a lot of effort and time to get right. Expect it to take a few months before you are playing comfortably and maybe longer before you can play well with others.

Look up as many song tabs as you can and play everything. Turn the radio on and try to copy songs you know by ear. Put the harp in a neck holder and play it with another instrument, do anything that will keep your interest piqued. Besides badly intonated toys the main reason for failure is simply not engaging enough. Music has never magically happened to anyone, we all have to put the time in. Most people who say "I can't do this" have simply not tried enough times.

You can often tell the difference between students who will or won't succeed. Those who have a drive and love music will usually figure it out eventually, while those who complain or sulk do not really get anywhere. No matter how bad the playing sounds, don't be the second type. Ignore fear, embarrassment, and failure and just chug ahead on your musical journey. Whether you play simple straight harp songs or learn to bend with crossharp people will love your playing. And you know what, even if they don't, who cares! Music is a creative expression, and it doesn't matter what others think. It is great for your health, breathing, memory, and will always get the attention of others. The harmonica has been played and loved for almost a couple hundred years now, there is clearly something about it that draws people. So, play your harp, mouth organ, pocket sax, tin sandwich, or whatever you call it. Play your harmonica and have fun!

Join the Symphony of Music Book Lovers!

If you've been captivated by the melodies in our pages, we've got a special note for you!

Subscribe to our exclusive mailing list for music book aficionados and be the first to get:

- Sneak peeks of upcoming books about your favorite artists and genres
- Exclusive interviews and stories from the music world
- Early access to special editions and book releases

Become Part of Our Melodic Community

Visit the link to Subscribe: https://bit.ly/3wZFjh2

OR

Scan the QR Code to Join Instantly:

Your email is a private backstage pass – no spam, just music. Ready to tune in?

Printed in Great Britain
by Amazon